FOR YOUR HOME

BABIES' & CHILDREN'S ROOMS

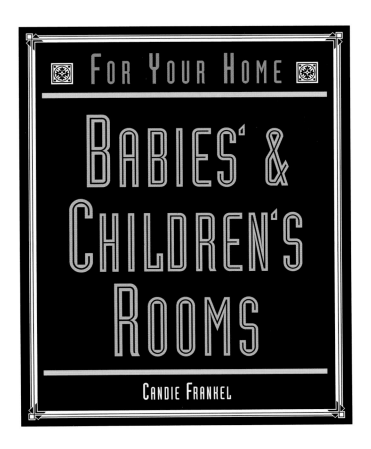

FOR YOUR HOME

BABIES' & CHILDREN'S ROOMS

Candie Frankel

Little, Brown and Company
Boston   New York   Toronto   London

DEDICATION

To Elizabeth Jane Wolotira

ACKNOWLEDGMENTS

The author gratefully acknowledges the many fine photographers and designers whose work is featured in these pages.

First edition

ISBN 0-316-29140-4

Library of Congress Catalog Card Number 94-73025

A FRIEDMAN GROUP BOOK

10 9 8 7 6 5 4 3 2 1

Published simultaneously in Canada by Little, Brown & Company (Canada) Limited

FOR YOUR HOME: BABIES' & CHILDREN'S ROOMS
was prepared and produced by
Michael Friedman Publishing Group, Inc.
15 West 26th Street
New York, New York 10010

Editor: Hallie Einhorn
Designer: Lynne Yeamans
Art Director: Jeff Batzli
Photography Editor: Emilya Naymark
Production Associate: Camille Lee

Color separations by Fine Arts Repro House Co., Ltd.
Printed in China by Leefung-Asco Printers Ltd.

TABLE OF CONTENTS

INTRODUCTION

No sooner does a baby become part of a family than all kinds of new and unfamiliar objects start filtering into the home. Furniture, clothing, toys, and books—all geared to a young child's growing body and mind—play an important role in making the home a welcome, nurturing place. Containing the accoutrements of childhood and organizing them so that they are accessible is a challenge all families face, especially if space is limited or shared.

When children inhabit a room, the decor is never static or "finished." A child's fast-as-a-beanstalk growth calls out for space that is flexible and adaptable. Furnishings must be able to accommodate evolving interests, new hobbies, and increasingly sophisticated tastes without resorting to an expensive decorating overhaul every time a change is desired. Young children need space to explore lots of different art, craft, and play activities at whim. They love the sense of mastery that scaled-down furniture and easy-to-reach shelves and cupboards give them.

Older children find the most use for hobby and study areas, as well as places to entertain friends. They don't want their rooms to appear babyish or out of sync with their personalities.

CHOOSING AN APPROACH

Planning a room that will grow with a child requires meeting present needs yet always keeping an eye on ways the room can be adapted in the future. For budget-conscious families, this typically means a onetime investment in sturdy, functional, module-type furniture that can serve from infancy through the teen years and beyond. The same storage cubes that stack an infant's diapers, for example, can be used later to stow playthings, socks, or a comic book collection. Using plain, well-designed furniture as a backdrop for a child's revolving collection of clothing, toys, and school supplies is the most economical way to keep a bedroom up-to-date.

Opposite: THE RIGHT FURNISHINGS AND LAYOUT CAN MAXIMIZE THE SPACE OF A SMALL ROOM. WITH THE HELP OF A RAISED BED AND STRATEGICALLY PLACED SHELVES, THIS LESS-THAN-SPACIOUS BEDROOM CONTAINS ALL OF A YOUNG CHILD'S NECESSITIES, INCLUDING AMPLE FLOOR SPACE FOR PLAY, A DESK FOR PROJECTS, AND PLENTY OF STORAGE FOR BOOKS, GAMES, AND TOYS. VISUALLY APPEALING AS WELL AS EFFICIENT, THE ROOM IS FILLED WITH WARM AND INVITING COLORS.

The sheer volume of possessions children accumulate tends to focus attention on their storage needs, but that is only part of the decorating story. Children live in a tactile world; they love to touch, hold, and handle, drinking in the essence of objects around them. Rather than keep precious objects off-limits, some parents feel that childhood is the best time to get acquainted with antique dolls, toys, and other valued items so that children can learn to appreciate and care for them. How lavishly a child's room incorporates expensive or rare objects is really a matter of personal style, time, budget, physical space, and child-rearing philosophy.

Parents with a keen aesthetic sense need to keep in mind that the types of rooms children consider successful and desirable may not look comfortable or inviting to adults. Children are proud of their possessions and like to keep them visible and accessible, which often means that shelves appear as a jumbled display of shapes and colors. The strong appeal of playhouses, giant stuffed animals, and beds that look like cars can be bewildering to adults, but items like these can mean a world of fun and fantasy to children. To create a room that is acceptable to both you and your child, start where all designers do: interview the client.

INVOLVING THE CHILD

Talking one-on-one with a child about the room he or she envisions is the first step toward refining the ideas both of you have. Children can be remarkably matter-of-fact when asked direct questions. They will tell you what colors they like, how and where they want to store their toys and books, and which kind of desk surface they prefer. Almost all have a fantasy bed in mind that would make their dream room complete. Looking at magazine pictures and visiting furniture and home decorating centers together can help you both visualize the possibilities and see what's new in the marketplace. If necessary, your comments can steer a budding designer in the right direction. You might point out, for example, that black is rarely used for walls and ceilings, but that it can look quite dramatic in an accent piece such as a lamp or poster.

Don't be afraid to be realistic with children about space and budget restrictions. Once you have a basic idea of the room's furniture requirements, measure the room together and draw a floor plan to scale on graph paper. Be sure to indicate the placement of windows, doors, electrical outlets, radiators, and air-conditioning vents. Small color cutouts, also to scale, can represent chests, desks, bookshelves, and beds. Children will enjoy working

with the "helicopter view" that a floor plan offers, and they can move the furniture cutouts around in order to try out a variety of possible arrangements.

Rather than immediately reject a request for a special piece of furniture, go over the budget available for the project with your child. Explain what different aspects of the new room (furniture, linens, paints, wallpaper) will cost so that you can decide together how best to allocate the money. In order to spread out the costs or purchase a special piece, you may opt to postpone some parts of the project until later. Even children who are generally spendthrift will rise to the challenge of creating a balanced, workable budget to achieve their decorating goals, and they will gain practical experience in arith-

metic, handling money, and comparison shopping in the process.

Children lead such vital, creative lives that they are the natural source for insight into their own space and storage requirements. When fulfilling these needs, the adults responsible for outfitting children's rooms must strive beyond the merely decorative to achieve flexibility. The rooms on the pages that follow are as unique as their individual owners and reflect variables such as budget, space, and the children's ages and special interests. Some of the ideas are readily practical and attainable, while others are fanciful springboards for the imagination. All can be applied alone or in combination to turn any child's ordinary, so-so room into a spectacular place to live, work, and play.

Above: BUILDING THE DECOR OF A CHILD'S ROOM AROUND A POPULAR THEME OR STORYBOOK CHARACTER NEEDN'T COST A FORTUNE IF PURCHASES ARE CHOSEN JUDICIOUSLY. A COLORFUL POSTER AND A FEW STUFFED-ANIMAL FRIENDS (ONE BEHIND THE WHEEL OF A HANDSOME RED CAR) WERE SUFFICIENT TO ESTABLISH THE BABAR THEME IN THIS COLORFUL BEDROOM. AS THE CHILD MATURES AND INTERESTS CHANGE, THE WHITE WALLS AND CONTEMPORARY WHITE DAYBED WILL FORM THE BACKDROP FOR A NEW LOOK, WHICH CAN BE ACHIEVED BY INTRODUCING A BEDCOVER, A WINDOW TREATMENT, AND PILLOWS IN NEW FABRICS AND COLORS.

WEE SPACES

Bringing a new baby home is such a special event that it's hard to resist setting up a grand nursery. Lavish canopied cribs, infant dressers, changing tables, and armloads of stuffed animals add so much charm to the new arrival's room, it hardly seems to matter that all these elements are quickly outgrown. However, while a separate nursery set aside for the new baby is always welcome, even families with space to spare often prefer to set up baby's area in the master bedroom for the first few months.

Despite popular buying trends, infants don't really need a lot of furnishings, clothing, accessories, or space to be happy. Most important are a sturdy, safe crib and, for parents and other caregivers, a comfortable chair for feedings as well as a changing table that is at a convenient height. Baby's clothing can be stored in armoires or other "grown-up" furniture, saving the expense of infant furniture that the baby will never personally use anyway.

White, ecru, and pastels are the most popular palettes for infants' rooms, but accents in bright primary colors are available too. Infants are more interested in light and shadow than in actual colors, so you might as well select bedding and accents in patterns you like while concentrating on keeping the room bright and cheery for baby.

The pages that follow show spaces that have been made comfortable and welcoming for infants and those who care for them. The ideas range from grand nurseries with every amenity to simple, cheerful setups in a spare room or corner. Each one is considerate of the basic needs of the wee ones who will call these places home.

Opposite: AN END OF A MASTER BEDROOM SUITE CAN BE READILY CONVERTED INTO A CONVENIENT TEMPORARY NURSERY. HERE, A MIRRORED CHIFFOROBE PROVIDES ATTRACTIVE STORAGE FOR BABY'S LAYETTE IN MULTIPLE DRAWERS AND CUPBOARDS. A WHITE WICKER CRIB HINTS AT THE GARDEN VIEW THAT CAN BE ENJOYED FROM THE SUNNY ENCLOSED PORCH ONLY A FEW STEPS BEYOND. **Above:** A FEW DECORATIVE EMBELLISHMENTS AND FURNISHINGS WERE THE SOLUTION FOR THIS OFFICE CONVERSION. FORMERLY A STUDY, THE STARK WHITE SPACE WAS SOFTENED WITH THE ADDITION OF PALE, HAND-PAINTED RIBBON AND FLORAL MOTIFS ON THE WALLS AND FLOOR. FURTHER EFFORTS TO MAKE THIS ROOM MORE COZY INCLUDED REPLACING VERTICAL BLINDS WITH FLOWING WHITE SWAGS AND COVERING THE CRIB AND CHANGING TABLE WITH FLORAL-PRINT LINENS.

Below: ANGLING A CRIB NEAR A DORMER WINDOW GIVES BABY PLENTY OF NATURAL FILTERED LIGHT WITHOUT BLOCKING ACCESS TO THE WINDOW SEAT. AN UPHOLSTERED CHAIR, USED FOR SNUGGLING AND FEEDING, IS ALSO STRATEGICALLY PLACED, FINDING A COZY SPOT AGAINST A LOW WALL UNDER THE EAVES. THE PAINTED MURAL ON THE ARMOIRE DOORS PROVIDES AN EXPANDED VISTA IN THIS SMALL BUT PLEASANT ROOM.

Above: TWO ADJOINING ROOMS IN A MASTER SUITE, EACH OPENING ONTO A COMMON HALL, ARE INGENIOUSLY SEPARATED BY A CANOPIED CRIB. THE CRIB FITS PERFECTLY UNDER THE WIDE ARCHED OPENING BETWEEN THE PARENTS' BEDROOM AND SITTING ROOM—TURNED-NURSERY, MAKING IT ACCESSIBLE FROM EITHER SIDE. ALTHOUGH THE CRIB IS SITUATED IN THE MIDST OF TWO ROOMS, THE ABUNDANCE OF HANGINGS ON THE CRIB CANOPY HELPS CREATE A PRIVATE AREA FOR BABY.

Below: IN THIS MASTER BEDROOM, THE BASSINET IS POSITIONED SO BABY CAN GAZE AT AN ELEGANT GEOMETRIC STAR SUSPENDED IN A NEARBY WINDOW. SAFELY MOUNTED, THE GENTLY ROTATING STAR IS AS VISUALLY TANTALIZING AS ANY CRIB MOBILE. OTHER STARS ALSO APPEAR IN THIS QUIET, UNDERSTATED CORNER, LENDING A PLAYFUL TOUCH TO THE ROOM. A COUPLE OF TOYS ARE KEPT ON HAND NEXT TO THE BASSINET WHERE THEY CAN BE EASILY FOUND BY THE CAREGIVER AS NEEDED.

Above: CONVENIENT FOR STORING BABY'S TOILETRIES, A WALL-MOUNTED CABINET PUTS NECESSARY ITEMS AT ARM'S REACH WITHOUT CLUTTERING UP THE CHANGING TABLE. THE CLEVER HINGED DESIGN ALLOWS THE LOUVERED PANELS TO SWING OPEN AND OUT OF THE WAY SO TINY HANDS AREN'T ACCIDENTALLY PiNCHED. A FEW FAMILIAR FRIENDS HOVER AROUND THE AREA TO KEEP BABY COMPANY DURING CHANGES.

Above: WHITE LAMINATED FURNITURE LINED UP AGAINST A NURSERY WALL CAN HELP TO
STREAMLINE AND OPEN UP A NARROW SPACE. THE MODULAR UNITS CHOSEN FOR
THIS COMPACT BUT EFFICIENT NURSERY CAN BE REARRANGED IN DIFFERENT CONFIGURATIONS,
MAKING THEM A PRACTICAL INVESTMENT OVER THE LONG TERM.

Below: SECONDHAND FURNISHINGS FOUND LOCALLY DECORATE THE NURSERY OF A VACATION COTTAGE, SAVING A FAMILY THE TIME AND EXPENSE OF SHIPPING FURNITURE FROM HOME. BARGAINS INCLUDE A DISTINCTIVE WICKER DRESSER FOR STORING CLOTHING AND ACCESSORIES, A FRAMED DISPLAY SHELF FOR PLAYTHINGS AND CHEERFUL DECORATIVE OBJECTS, AND A QUILT STAND PERFECT FOR CRIB SHEETS AND BLANKETS. GATHERED FABRIC PANELS CAMOUFLAGE THE COTTAGE'S CRUMBLING WALLS UNTIL THEY CAN BE PROPERLY REPLASTERED.

Above: DURING A BEDROOM RENOVATION OR BUILDING PROJECT, THE NURSERY CAN BE RELOCATED TO A FAMILY LIVING AREA, SUCH AS A FRONT SITTING ROOM OR ENCLOSED PORCH. HERE, AN ANTIQUE CARRIAGE AND A STANDING LAMP WITH SHELVES HELP BLOCK THE ROOM'S WIDE FORMAL ENTRYWAY, MAKING THE SPACE MORE INTIMATE.

Opposite: A JUMBO YELLOW MOON AND COMPANION BLUE STARS PROVIDE AN INEXPENSIVE ANTIDOTE TO THE ALL-WHITE STERILITY THAT COMMONLY CHARACTERIZES AN INFANT'S ROOM. PLUSH BLUE CARPETING ANCHORS THE SOOTHING COLOR SCHEME. WITH AN EYE TOWARD THE FUTURE, THE PARENTS AVOIDED CUTE NURSERY LAMPS IN FAVOR OF WALL-MOUNTED, SWING-ARM LAMPS THAT CAN BE USED WHEN THE CHILD IS OLDER. THE TRADITIONAL ROCKING CHAIR, PERFECT FOR COAXING BABY TO SLEEP, WILL ALSO RETAIN A PLACE IN THE HOME AT A LATER DATE.

Above: CREATING AN ENERGETIC MOOD, A PALETTE OF BRILLIANT PRIMARY AND SECONDARY COLORS KEEPS THIS ROOM BRIGHT AND UPBEAT, EVEN ON OVERCAST DAYS. COLORFUL DETAILS INCLUDE CRIB BUMPER PADS, CHAIR AND STOOL CUSHIONS, FABRIC WALL ART, AND PLASTIC DRAWER PULLS. THE IVORY WALLS AND LIGHT TAUPE CARPETING ARE UNDERSTATED AND NEUTRAL IN TONE, ALLOWING THE VIBRANT COLORS TO JUMP OUT.

Above: NATURAL WOOD AND WICKER FURNISHINGS ECHO THE COLORS AND THEMES OF THIS WILDLIFE MURAL. THE CRIB HAS BEEN STRATEGICALLY PLACED SO THAT BABY CAN SEE THE BLACK-AND-WHITE PANDAS UP CLOSE; THE SHARP CONTRAST BETWEEN BLACK AND WHITE IS KNOWN TO FASCINATE INFANTS AND HELP DEVELOP THEIR FOCUSING SKILLS. AS THE BABY GROWS INTO TODDLERHOOD, THE OTHER ANIMALS IN THE ROOM WILL BECOME FAMILIAR FRIENDS AS WELL. **Opposite:** THIS COORDINATED NURSERY SUITE HAS BEEN EASILY CREATED BY PAINTING OLD UNFINISHED FURNITURE WHITE TO MATCH THE CRIB. AS NEEDS CHANGE, ADDITIONAL PIECES CAN BE REVIVED AND ADDED IN A SIMILAR FASHION. THE LIFELIKE BABY GIRAFFE, WITH ITS DARK, NATURAL TONES, STANDS OUT AGAINST THE WHITE FURNITURE, PREVENTING THE ENSEMBLE FROM APPEARING BLAND OR WASHED OUT; THIS ENORMOUS STUFFED ANIMAL IS ALSO AN ENTERTAINING COMPANION FOR BABY.

WORK AND PLAY

The bedroom of an active, inquisitive child is far more than a place to sleep—it also serves as a laboratory, library, art studio, study, backstage dressing area, and construction zone. As children undertake the serious business of play, they develop motor skills, embark on projects, role-play, and learn how to negotiate. The successful room functions as part workshop, part showcase. It gives a child the freedom to try all sorts of activities, to show off accomplishments and collections, and to pursue new avenues as interests change. When there is more than one child in the family, a shared play-room can provide many of these same functions.

Parents can help children get their rooms on the right track by providing large, smooth work surfaces and am-

ple lighting. Tables, desks, and chairs should be at a comfortable height appropriate to the child's age and size. Movable furniture should be lightweight so that children can rearrange it as needed or clear the decks entirely for an impromptu dance. For young children, the floor is an important surface for play. Hardwood or tile floors are best for blocks, puzzles, and toys with wheels, while plush carpeting invites sprawling out for reading or playing a board game.

The following pages reveal rooms that indulge children's special interests and hobbies, from doll collecting to space travel. Each one carries its own imprimatur and offers valuable ideas for display techniques, storage, work surfaces, and overall decor.

Opposite: DOLLS AND STUFFED ANIMALS ARE READY FOR IMAGINATIVE PLAY AT A MOMENT'S NOTICE IN THIS TODDLER'S ROOM. THE PALE PEACH TINT CHOSEN FOR THE WALLS AND WARDROBE IS WARMER THAN PLAIN WHITE, YET STILL FUNCTIONS AS A NEUTRAL BACKGROUND FOR THE ROOM'S ECLECTIC COLLECTION. CHILD-SIZE CHAIRS AND A RUG WITH WOVEN ANIMAL FIGURES DRAW ATTENTION TO THE FLOOR, WHERE MUCH OF CHILDREN'S PLAY OCCURS. Above: A LARGE BULLETIN BOARD, AMPLE BUILT-IN STORAGE, AND SOPHISTICATED MIDNIGHT BLUE CARPETING WILL USHER THE TODDLER OCCUPANT OF THIS ROOM INTO THE STUDENT YEARS WITH EASE. IN THE MEANTIME, THERE IS PLENTY OF ROOM FOR BOTH ACTIVE AND QUIET PLAY. THE SWING-GATE CRIB WILL SOON BE REPLACED BY A JUNIOR BED.

Left: A STEP-UP CARPETED PLATFORM PROVIDES A DISTINCT PLAY AREA THAT IS EASILY TRANSFORMED INTO A STAGE FOR REHEARSED OR IMPROMPTU THEATRICAL PERFORMANCES. GRACING EITHER SIDE OF THE THEATER'S CENTER AISLE ARE TWIN BEDS THAT PROVIDE COMFORTABLE SEATING FOR AUDIENCES OF ALL AGES. THE JABOT-STYLED WINDOW TREATMENT CARRIES OUT THE THESPIAN THEME, WHILE A NARROW PARTITION CONCEALS A SMALL BACKSTAGE DRESSING AREA.

Right: OUT-OF-THE-ORDINARY FURNISHINGS CAN INSPIRE A FESTIVE, PARTYLIKE MOOD IN A CHILD'S ROOM ALMOST INSTANTLY. HERE, A COLORFUL CANOPY IS DRAPED ACROSS THE CEILING, SUGGESTING THE FUN AND EXCITEMENT OF A VISIT TO THE CIRCUS. THE ROOM'S PROPORTIONS ARE TURNED ON END, ALICE-IN-WONDERLAND STYLE, WITH THE ADDITION OF TWO GIANT (BUT MAKE-BELIEVE) CRAYONS. A YOUNG ARTIST CAN SIT DOWN TO SOME SERIOUS COLORING IN THIS ROOM AT ANY TIME BY SIMPLY TEARING SOME FRESH PAPER OFF THE HANDY WALL-MOUNTED ROLL.

Above: RAINY DAYS AREN'T QUITE SO DISAPPOINTING IN A BEDROOM WITH AN OUTDOOR THEME. A STRIPED AWNING VALANCE, IVY-PLANTED WINDOW BOX, AND GARDEN-FRESH WICKER FURNITURE ALLOW YOUNG LADIES TO ENJOY A TEA PARTY ON A PRETEND PATIO. SHOULD IT START TO RAIN, THEY CAN ALWAYS RUN TO THE FANTASY-HOUSE BED FOR SHELTER.

Opposite: TRANSPORTATION THEMES REIGN SUPREME IN THIS LONDON BEDROOM, LEAVING NO DOUBT AS TO A YOUNG BOY'S MOST SERIOUS PASSION. THE FREESTANDING RED BUNK IS A FUN STAND-IN FOR A DOUBLE-DECKER BUS, PROVIDING HOURS OF ENTERTAINMENT, AS WELL AS A COMFORTABLE PLACE TO SLEEP, FOR OWNER AND VISITING PLAYMATES ALIKE. IMITATING REAL LIFE TO THE MINUTEST DETAIL, THIS FANTASY BUS TRAVELS A PAVED ROAD CLEVERLY SIMULATED BY A LIGHT GRAY CARPET INSET.

Above: A RAISED PLATFORM PLAYHOUSE AT THE OTHER END OF THE LONDON BEDROOM PROVIDES A SECURE HOME FOR A LARGE FAMILY OF STUFFED ANIMALS. LARGE PULLOUT DRAWERS AT THE BASE OF THE HOUSE STORE OTHER TOYS AND MAKE CLEANUP AFTER FLOOR PLAY AN EASY CHORE. BY INCORPORATING FAMILIAR SIGHTS INTO THE DECOR, THE ROOM MAKES THE REAL CITY SEEM LESS OVERWHELMING AND EASIER TO NAVIGATE.

Opposite: OVERNIGHT GUESTS ARE PART OF THE ROUTINE IN THIS LIVELY ROOM CONTAINING TWO BUNK BEDS. THE L-SHAPED CONFIGURATION ALLOWS A SINGLE LADDER TO SERVE BOTH UPPER BERTHS. SUSPENDED FROM HIGH RAFTERS, AN INDOOR SWING IS A DEFINITE VISITOR ATTRACTION. OTHER SOURCES OF ENTERTAINMENT, SUCH AS COSTUMES AND TOYS, AS WELL AS PERSONAL MEMENTOS LINE THE WALLS AND OVERMANTEL, LEAVING THE CARPETED FLOOR FREE FOR PLAY.

Above: TO TONE DOWN AN INTENSE PRIMARY PALETTE, FABRICS WITH A STONEWASHED DENIM HUE FILL IN FOR BRIGHT ROYAL BLUE. USED ON THE WALLS AND BEDCOVERS, THE PALER BLUE TINT VISUALLY RECEDES, CAUSING THE BRIGHT RED AND YELLOW ACCENTS TO POP OUT. EXTRA FLOOR SPACE IS GAINED BY THE DOUBLE-STACKED BUNKS—A TIME-HONORED ARRANGEMENT WHEN SIBLINGS SHARE A ROOM.

Below: A WIDE PARTNERS DESK OFFERS A GENEROUS WORK SURFACE FOR THE SERIOUS STUDENT OR ARTIST. EXTREMELY USEFUL, THIS TYPE OF DESK PERMITS THE OWNER AND A FRIEND TO PULL UP CHAIRS ON EITHER SIDE FOR A MARATHON STUDY SESSION, AN INTENSE BOARD GAME, OR AN IMPORTANT CONSULTATION. THE DESK'S U-SHAPED END HELPS TO SOFTEN THE MANY ANGULAR LINES OF THIS BEDROOM'S SHELVES AND STORAGE UNITS.

Above: A PINE TABLE-AND-CHAIR SET PLACED IN FRONT OF OPEN VERANDA DOORS ALLOWS A YOUNG ARTIST TO ENJOY A SUMMER BREEZE. JOINING THE IMPROMPTU COLORING SESSION ARE SNOOPY (IN CELEBRITY SHADES) AND A DELICATE CHINA DOLL. ALTHOUGH THE HOSTESS HAS TEMPORARILY ABANDONED HER GUESTS, THE PLETHORA OF ENTICING CRAYONS AND COLORING BOOKS SUGGESTS THAT SHE WILL SOON RETURN TO FINISH HER MASTERPIECE.

Below: MODELED AFTER PROFESSIONAL DRAFTING TABLES, AN ANGLED, ADJUSTABLE WORK SURFACE GIVES A BEDROOM A CRISP ENGINEERED APPEARANCE. A GRID BEHIND THE DESK CAN BE USED TO DISPLAY AWARD RIBBONS AND PHOTOGRAPHS, WHILE STEEL SHELVES ABOVE HELP TO ORGANIZE GAMES, SPORTS EQUIPMENT, AND HOBBY SUPPLIES. THE FLOATING-BED DESIGN AND RAISED DESK DRAWERS HELP THIS SMALL ROOM APPEAR LARGER BY EXPOSING ADDITIONAL FLOOR SPACE. AS POSSESSIONS ACCUMULATE, THESE AREAS CAN PROVIDE EFFICIENT, OUT-OF-THE-WAY STORAGE.

Above: PURSUING HOBBIES IN A SMALL ROOM IS MADE EASIER WITH AN L-SHAPED DESK LIKE THOSE USED IN PROFESSIONAL BUSINESS OFFICES. AN OBJECT OR PROJECT CAN BE PLACED ON ONE ARM OF THE DESK, WHILE A REFERENCE TEXT OR INSTRUCTION MANUAL RESTS ON THE OTHER. BOTH CAN REMAIN IN EASY VIEW AND BE CONSULTED WITHOUT FRUSTRATING RESHUFFLING. A FREESTANDING SHELF EXTENDS THE UNIT SHOWN HERE, GIVING THE OWNER A PLACE TO DISPLAY MODEL ROCKETS AND OTHER TREASURES.

Above: A WINDOWED ALCOVE LEADING TO A PRIVATE BATHROOM SUGGESTED THE PERFECT

OUT-OF-THE-WAY STUDY CORNER. RECEIVING PLENTY OF NATURAL LIGHT, IT IS AN IDEAL LOCATION FOR HOURS OF

DILIGENT STUDY. THE QUIET NOOK OFFERS A MEASURE OF PRIVACY, WHICH IS A REAL ASSET IN A

WELL-ORGANIZED SHARED ROOM SUCH AS THIS. AT THE SAME TIME, THE DESK'S BOLD RED COLOR SERVES AS A

DECORATIVE PLOY TO HELP DRAW THE ALCOVE BACK INTO THE ROOM SO THAT THE SPACE DOESN'T

APPEAR QUITE SO ALOOF. **Right:** WHEN A PRIVATE STUDY AREA IS NOT FEASIBLE, SEQUESTERING A DESK CAN

BE AN EXCELLENT ALTERNATIVE. THIS SEMIPRIVATE STUDY AREA IS DEFINED BY A BACKYARD PLAYHOUSE,

PAINTED WHITE AND BROUGHT INDOORS. WHILE NOT SOUNDPROOF OR COMPLETELY PRIVATE, THE SPACE DOES

SURROUND A YOUNG SCHOLAR AND ENCOURAGE CONCENTRATION. CUT PAPER CURTAINS PRESENT

A CHEERFUL WELCOME AT THE ENTRANCE.

Below: MANY WORLDS COLLIDE IN THIS COLORFUL ROOM, WHICH IS RIPE FOR FANTASY AND PLAY. THE FLOOR PLAY AREA IS DELIBERATELY KEPT FREE, ALLOWING THE ALTERNATING SOLID AND PATTERNED CARPET TO SUGGEST TERRITORIES FOR SUPERHERO ESCAPADES. A SCALED-DOWN VERSION OF A CLASSIC IRON BEDSTEAD AND A LOW TABLE WITH CHAIRS KEEP EVERYTHING GEARED TO THE LEVEL OF THE TODDLER RESIDENT. A THREE-STEP STAIRCASE, PAINTED BRIGHT RED, MAKES AN UNUSUAL TIP-PROOF NIGHTSTAND.

Above: ADULT-SIZE CLOSETS MAKE LITTLE SENSE IF TODDLERS AREN'T ABLE TO REACH THE ITEMS STORED INSIDE. IN THIS BEDROOM, THE DOORS OF AN UNDERUTILIZED CLOSET WERE REMOVED, AND THE CLOSET INTERIOR WAS TRANSFORMED INTO A CHEERY RED NOOK. THE NOOK PRESENTLY SERVES AS A BACKDROP FOR A PLAY KITCHEN BUT IT COULD JUST AS EASILY ACCOMMODATE OTHER PLAYTHINGS, SUCH AS TRICYCLES AND WAGONS, AN EASEL AND ART SUPPLIES, OR BOOKS ON LOW SHELVES.

Below: FOR NOW, THIS HANDSOME UPPER-STORY SPACE IS USED AS A PLAYROOM, BUT IT IS DESTINED FOR A GLAMOROUS FUTURE. THE ELEGANT WINDOW TREATMENT, HAND-PAINTED CABINET, AND RICH CARPETING ARE BUT FIRST INSTALLMENTS IN THE MORE TRADITIONAL DECOR THAT WILL APPEAR AS THE CHILDREN OUTGROW THEIR PLAYHOUSE, TOY KITCHEN, AND TINY TABLE AND STOOLS.

Above: IN TWO- AND THREE-STORY HOMES, KEEPING TOTS AWAY FROM STAIRWELLS IS A SERIOUS CHALLENGE. ONE TIME-HONORED SOLUTION IS A SAFETY GATE AT THE TOP OF THE STAIRS, SHOWN HERE IN AN ATTRACTIVE PICKET-FENCE DESIGN THAT HAS ROUNDED EDGES ON TOP FOR SAFETY. WITH THE GATE CLOSED, THE STAIRWELL LEADING DOWN FROM THIS SUNNY ATTIC PLAYROOM IS SAFELY OUT OF BOUNDS, YET THE OPEN DESIGN ALLOWS YOUNGSTERS TO REMAIN IN FULL EARSHOT OF THE FLOOR BELOW.

Below: SKYLIGHTS BRING MUCH-NEEDED LIGHT INTO AN ATTIC CONVERSION THAT HAS ONLY ONE WINDOW. THIS UPPER-STORY PLAYROOM RELEGATES THE CHILDREN'S ACTIVITIES AND CLUTTER TO ONE FLOOR OF THE HOUSE, AWAY FROM THE FAMILY'S MAIN LIVING AREA. RATHER THAN FEELING BANISHED, THE CHILDREN DELIGHT IN ESCAPING TO THEIR OWN PRIVATE WORLD. PLUSH GREEN CARPETING SUGGESTS THE SOFT MOSSY EARTH FOUND IN WOODLANDS.

Above: ENCOURAGING CHILDREN TO DEVELOP THEIR CREATIVE POWERS, THE OPPOSITE END OF THIS PLAYROOM FEATURES A PUPPET THEATER AND CHILD-SIZE BOX OFFICE. THE TRIFOLD PARTITION IS SAFELY ANCHORED AND PADDED WITH CARPETING. PROVIDING PLENTY OF STORAGE FOR PUPPETS AND PROPS, SHELVES AND CUBBYHOLES BEHIND THE PARTITION EXTEND THE PLAY AREA FOR YOUNG THEATER MANAGERS.

Above: THE SPECIAL REQUEST OF A LITTLE GIRL INSPIRED THIS PLAYHOUSE BED,

RENDERED FEASIBLE BY THE BEDROOM'S HIGH CEILINGS. REAL HOUSE DETAILS

INCLUDE GINGERBREAD SCALLOPS, LOUVERED SHUTTERS, AND A SHINGLED CEDAR ROOF.

COMPLETING THE OUTDOOR ILLUSION ARE A LANDSCAPE MURAL, A SKY BLUE

CEILING, AND GRASS-GREEN CARPETING, ALL OF WHICH BRING THE JOYS OF SUMMERTIME

TO EVEN THE COLDEST WINTER DAYS.

CREATIVE STORAGE

Ample accessible storage is the key to creating a well-organized room that a child can keep tidy without an adult's prodding. Most children take readily to sorting and organizing tasks, but they usually give up when drawers stick or are too heavy, shelves are packed too full, or closet rods are too high to reach. Easy-glide drawers, see-through plastic bins, and stackable baskets are inexpensive items that show thoughtful consideration for a child's size, strength, and patience. Shelves positioned at a child's level are a must for books, games, and puzzles that are used frequently. Like adults, children function more efficiently when everything they need is well organized and at their fingertips. Good storage lets youngsters move intently from one activity to the next and makes cleanup go faster, with less frustration.

Designing suitable storage requires analyzing a room's size and present furnishings, and mapping out possibilities for new storage on a floor plan. Even the smallest bedroom has underutilized space that can be tapped for its storage potential. The pages that follow show a variety of storage solutions, including dual-purpose furniture, under-bed storage, wire shelving, and window seats. Some units are built-in while others are freestanding. All dramatically increase storage space while enhancing the decor.

Opposite: A CUSTOM-BUILT FLOOR-TO-CEILING STORAGE WALL PROVIDES A TEENAGER WITH PLENTY OF SPACE FOR SPORTING EQUIPMENT AND CLOTHING. OUT-OF-SEASON ITEMS ARE STORED IN THE TOP CABINETS, AND EVERYTHING IS ROTATED AS THE SEASONS CHANGE TO GIVE EASY DAILY ACCESS. CUBBYHOLES ABOVE THE BUILT-IN DESK SORT BOOKS, PAPERS, AND SOUVENIRS. **Above:** IN A SHARED BEDROOM REQUIRING A LOT OF FURNITURE, TRIM WHITE MODULAR UNITS CAN PREVENT A JUMBLED, OVERCROWDED LOOK. THE WHITE PIECES IN THIS BEDROOM—BUNK BEDS WITH A TRUNDLE UNDERNEATH, MID-HEIGHT DOUBLE BOOKCASES, A WIDE-TOP DESK, AND A NIGHTSTAND—BLEND SEAMLESSLY INTO THE WHITE WALL BACKGROUND. THE SAME FURNITURE IN DARKER COLORS OR WOOD TONES WOULD BE MORE OBTRUSIVE AND MAKE THE SPACE LOOK SMALLER.

Below: SOMETIMES LOOKING NO FURTHER THAN A FURNITURE RETAILER'S SHOWROOM CAN YIELD THE STORAGE OPTION THAT'S BEST FOR A PARTICULAR ROOM. HERE, A PAIR OF TALL DRAWER-AND-SHELF UNITS FILLS IN FOR NIGHTSTANDS ON EITHER SIDE OF A TWIN BED, ADDING FEET OF WELCOME STORAGE IN AN UNEXPECTED PLACE. TO PREVENT THE UNITS FROM OVERWHELMING AND DWARFING THE BED, THE SAME BRIGHT RED HUE WAS CHOSEN FOR THE COVERLET. A RECESSED AREA BEHIND THE BED MAKES THE PERFECT NEST FOR A STUFFED-ANIMAL MENAGERIE.

Above: BUILDING A COMBINATION BUNK BED AND STORAGE PLATFORM IN THE MIDDLE OF A BEDROOM CREATED A MORE PRIVATE ARRANGEMENT FOR TWO SISTERS WHO SHARE THE SPACE. THE BUNKS OPEN OUT ONTO OPPOSITE SIDES AND AT DIFFERENT LEVELS, GIVING EACH GIRL HER OWN DRESSING AREA AND STORAGE FOR PERSONAL THINGS. KEEPING THE LINES OF COMMUNICATION OPEN, A WINDOW IN THE BACK WALL OF EACH BUNK ALLOWS FOR ACROSS-THE-ROOM CONVERSATION AND PROVIDES VENTILATION.

Above: A SLEEPING ALCOVE CARVED OUT OF A FORMER CLOSET MIMICS THE BOX AND CLOSET BEDS TRADITIONAL IN NORTHERN CLIMATES. SHELVES AT THE HEAD AND FOOT OF THE BED ARE PARTIALLY HIDDEN FROM VIEW, KEEPING THE MAIN PLAY AREA FREE OF CLUTTER. TO KEEP OUT EARLY-MORNING LIGHT OR SIMPLY TO PROVIDE SOME PRIVACY, A FOAM INSERT CAN BE SLIPPED INTO THE CRESCENT WINDOW FRAME.

Above: TWO CLOSELY SPACED WINDOWS IN THIS CORNER BEDROOM CROWDED IN ON A CONVENTIONAL TWIN BED,

NO MATTER WHICH WAY IT WAS POSITIONED. TO RESOLVE THE FLOOR-PLAN DILEMMA, COMPACT BUILT-IN FURNITURE

WAS DESIGNED. THESE PIECES INCORPORATE BOTH WINDOWS INTO THE OVERALL DESIGN, FLANKING ONE WITH NARROW

DISPLAY SHELVES AND GIVING THE OTHER A WINDOW SEAT WITH STORAGE. STURDY CROSS-BRACES JOINING THE BED'S

TOPMOST RAILS LAY THE GROUNDWORK FOR UPPER STORAGE CABINETS TO BE INSTALLED AT A LATER DATE.

Right: AN INNOVATIVE BUNK BED ARRANGEMENT CAN MAXIMIZE STORAGE IN A LONG, NARROW SPACE. HERE, THE LOWER BUNK'S PLATFORM EXTENDS THE FULL LENGTH OF THE ROOM, PROVIDING A SMOOTH, FLAT PLAY SURFACE ABOVE A SINGLE BANK OF DEEP DRAWERS. THE SUPPORT STRUCTURE FOR THE UPPER BUNK PROVIDES STORAGE SHELVES IN ADDITION TO THE REQUIRED LADDER. ALTHOUGH MUCH ATTENTION HAS BEEN DEVOTED TO THE PRACTICAL EFFICIENCY OF THIS ROOM, THE AESTHETIC ASPECT HAS NOT BEEN OVERLOOKED. REFLECTING THE CHEERFUL SPONTANEITY OF CHILDHOOD, THE WALLPAPER AND LINENS SHOW OFF RANDOM, BRIGHT HAND- AND FOOTPRINT DESIGNS REMINISCENT OF A CHILD'S FINGER PAINTING.

Left: REACHED BY A SHORT, EASY-TO-CLIMB LADDER, THIS MID-HEIGHT PLATFORM BED PACKS LOTS OF STORAGE SPACE UNDERNEATH AND HOUSES A SIZEABLE LIBRARY ON SHELVES ABOVE. CONVENIENTLY LOCATED ONLY A FEW STEPS FROM THE BOOK COLLECTION, A COZY EASY CHAIR PROVIDES MUCH-APPRECIATED COMFORT FOR THE BEDTIME STORYTELLER. THE BED, OVERHUNG WITH A DECORATIVE CANOPY, HAS THE ADDED ADVANTAGE OF BED CURTAINS THAT CAN BE DRAWN CLOSED FOR COMPLETE SECLUSION.

Above: A SLANTING CEILING THAT CUTS BACK OPTIONS FOR FREESTANDING FURNITURE OFTEN PROVIDES THE PERFECT SITE FOR A BUILT-IN DESK. HERE, THE BANK OF CABINETS SUPPORTING THE LONG COUNTER ADDS PRECIOUS INCHES OF STORAGE IN A SMALL BEDROOM, WHILE STILL LEAVING AMPLE ROOM FOR A DESK KNEEHOLE. WITH PLENTY OF SPACE FOR PAPERS, BOOKS, AND SCIENCE PROJECTS, THE VAST WORK SURFACE EASILY ACCOMMODATES A COMPUTER MONITOR AND KEYBOARD AS WELL. **Right:** ASYMMETRICAL BUILT-IN FURNITURE PREVENTS A BEDROOM ALCOVE FROM APPEARING STILTED OR PREDICTABLE. THIS UNIT INCLUDES A WARDROBE AND UNDER-BED STORAGE DRAWERS, ELIMINATING THE NEED FOR A SEPARATE DRESSER AND NIGHT TABLE. UP ABOVE, THE SLOPED CEILING RISES IN AN ARCHITECTURAL CANOPY.

Opposite: TIRED OF HAVING STUFFED TOYS DOMINATE HIS ROOM BUT NOT QUITE WILLING TO PART WITH THEM, A YOUNG COLLECTOR HAS GATHERED THEM IN A JUMBO WICKER FRUIT BASKET. THESE CHERISHED SOURCES OF COMFORT ARE AVAILABLE FOR QUICK HUGS WHEN A NOSTALGIC PANG TAKES OVER, BUT MOST OF THE TIME THEY ARE HIDDEN FROM VIEW IN HIS NEWER, MORE GROWN-UP ROOM. **Above:** INSPIRED BY THE ROLLING CARTS USED ON FACTORY FLOORS, TOY BINS ON WHEELS ARE PRACTICAL FOR STORING POSSESSIONS AND MOVING THEM AROUND A BEDROOM. AFTER PLAY, YOUNGSTERS CAN ROLL AN EMPTY BIN OVER TO THE PLAY AREA AND PILE THEIR TOYS INTO IT, MAKING THE TIDYING-UP PROCESS FAST AND UNCOMPLICATED. TO INCREASE FLOOR SPACE, EACH BIN HAS ITS OWN GARAGE BUILT INTO THE WALL UNIT.

Above: Open metal shelving purchased at a kitchen supply store forms an impressive storage bank in a boy's bedroom. Books, models, and stuffed toys occupy the upper shelves, while down below, rigs are ready to pull out at a moment's notice. A trifold louvered screen garages a few additional items behind the bed. **Right:** Mustard gold steel shelving units partition this large room into two distinct areas. Baby's side is simply furnished with a standard crib and a chest that doubles as a changing table. Just steps away, a sitting and craft area allows mother to pursue personal interests while still being able to keep a close eye on baby. Color-coded plastic crates, which make great, inexpensive organizational tools, line the partitioning shelves, storing items for both areas.

Above: BANKING ALL THE SHELVES ON A WINDOW WALL MAKES A ROOM SEEM LARGER AND NEATER. IN THIS CITY APARTMENT, OPEN SHELVES BUILT AROUND AN EXISTING WINDOW HOLD GAMES, BOOKS, AND STUFFED ANIMALS. THE WINDOW HELPS DRAW THE EYE OUT, PAST SHELVES THAT ARE POTENTIALLY OVERFILLED OR SLIGHTLY DISORGANIZED. BALLOON SHADES AND A GAUZY BED CANOPY SOFTEN THE SHELVES' PRECISION GRID AND GIVE THE ROOM A COZY FEELING.

Below: PLASTIC STORAGE BOXES LETTERED WITH PERMANENT PEN KEEP THE SMALL BITS AND PIECES OF A YOUNGSTER'S VARIED COLLECTION PROPERLY SORTED AND CATALOGED. ADULT PERUSAL OF A CHILD'S ESSENTIAL CATEGORIES IS BOUND TO DRAW A SMILE AND PERHAPS A MEMORY OR TWO. THE BOXES ARE STACKED NEATLY IN AN OAK DISPLAY SHELF AND CAN EASILY BE RETRIEVED FOR CLOSE INSPECTION OF THE CONTENTS.

Above: A LIVING ROOM CORNER SET ASIDE FOR VISITING CHILDREN FEATURES A LOW BOOKSHELF FILLED WITH TOYS, BOOKS, AND GAMES. EVERYTHING STORED HERE ENCOURAGES QUIET PLAY AND INVITES THE CHILDREN TO AMUSE THEMSELVES WHILE THE GROWN-UPS ARE TALKING.

Opposite: PUTTING A COLLECTION ON FULL DISPLAY IS ONE WAY TO RESOLVE A STORAGE DILEMMA. FOLK ART CRITTERS AND FAMILY PHOTOS ARE AMONG THE MANY TREASURED ITEMS MOUNTED ON WALLS AND PERCHED ON SHELVES THROUGHOUT THIS LIVELY BEDROOM-TURNED—ART GALLERY. ADDITIONAL ITEMS ARE REFLECTED IN THE MIRROR ABOVE THE HEADBOARD.

Above: A JACKET AND SNEAKERS WORN EVERY DAY ARE EASILY FOUND HANGING OUT IN THE OPEN ON A PEGBOARD. NO PLAIN BOARD MODEL, THIS CRESCENT-SHAPED MAN-IN-THE-MOON PEGBOARD WAS CUT ON A JIGSAW AND HAND-PAINTED. CONTINUING THE CELESTIAL THEME, THE PALE BLUE WALL IS STENCILED AT RANDOM WITH WHITE STARS.

Above: ROBIN'S-EGG BLUE, A TRADITIONAL COLOR FOR CABINET INTERIORS, PERKS UP A BANK OF SERVICEABLE WHITE CABINETS AND ACCENTS THEIR DEPTH. ALTHOUGH THE STORAGE SPACE PROVIDED HERE IS AMPLE, MOST OF THE CONTENTS REMAIN HIDDEN FROM VIEW, A SENSIBLE APPROACH IN A SMALL ROOM THAT COULD EASILY BE OVERWHELMED BY TOO BUSY A DISPLAY. **Opposite:** LOOKING MORE LIKE A CASTLE THAN A STORAGE UNIT, THIS PIECE OF BEDROOM FURNITURE MAKES A GAME OUT OF TAKING OBJECTS OUT AND PUTTING THEM AWAY. THE CABINET DOORS SWING OPEN BY PULLING ON THE EASY-TO-SEE BAR HANDLES, BUT TODDLERS CAN ALSO REACH IN THROUGH THE RECTANGULAR AND ARCHED CUTOUT OPENINGS TO RETRIEVE WANTED TOYS. IN THE MIDDLE SECTION, OPEN SHELVES STORE ASSORTED TOYS IN FULL VIEW AND OFFER A SHELTERED DISPLAY AREA FOR WOODEN BLOCKS. SINCE CHILDREN CANNOT REACH THE TOP COMPARTMENTS, THESE AREAS ARE BEST RESERVED FOR SEASONAL TOYS AND CLOTHES.

GROWING UP

The threshold into young adulthood is never crossed overnight, though it may seem that way to a lot of parents. The bedrooms of older children are often curious mixtures of old and new, reflecting a stage of transition. Stuffed animals and other fond reminders of childhood mingle freely with sophisticated electronic equipment, sports paraphernalia, and celebrity posters. These are the years to pursue childhood interests in greater depth as well as to daydream and prepare for the future.

An increased need for privacy, a quiet, well-equipped study area, and room to entertain friends are all important aspects of an adolescent's world. The ideal bedroom functions like a small suite, giving independence and total privacy when desired yet remaining steps away from the hub of family activities. Newly developed tastes may lead an older child to demonstrate considerable decorating savvy when it comes to pursuing the colors, lighting, and furnishings needed for a particular ambience. The pages that follow contain ideas for surface finishes, window treatments, bedding, storage, and displays that can make any adolescent's room a haven from the world as well as a preparation for it.

Opposite: SHADES OF LAVENDER, PURPLE, AND ROSE CREATE A REGAL PALACE FOR A PETITE PRINCESS. THE BOUDOIR CHAIR IS AN ORDINARY DESK CHAIR DRAPED WITH PURPLE FABRIC AND FINISHED WITH A POUFY KNOT. THE LOW L-SHAPED DESK WITH ITS BAROQUE MIRROR IS JUST AS LIKELY TO BE USED FOR COLORING AS FOR APPLYING LIPSTICK BEFORE A DANCE RECITAL. A LATERAL FILE CABINET THAT HAS BEEN SPONGED SMOKY GRAY STORES VALUABLE POSSESSIONS UNDER LOCK AND KEY. **Above:** INDULGING A YOUNG PERSON'S INTEREST IN HISTORICAL OBJECTS CAN HELP FOSTER A LIFELONG APPRECIATION. THE OCCUPANT OF THIS BEDROOM IS THRILLED TO BE SLEEPING ON AN OLD IRON BEDSTEAD WITH AN ANTIQUE COUNTERPANE AND PATCHWORK QUILT. THE FLOWERY DECOR KEEPS THE FEELING OF SPRING ALIVE THROUGHOUT THE YEAR.

Below: A GIRL'S FIRST TRADITIONAL BEDROOM SUITE, SELECTED FROM THE JUVENILE DEPARTMENT, IS SCALED SLIGHTLY SMALLER THAN ADULT FURNITURE TO SUIT HER STILL-GROWING FRAME. THE FRENCH BED, WHICH FACES INTO THE ROOM LIKE A COUCH, GIVES THE ROOM THE AURA OF A LADY'S PARLOR. LOUVERED SHUTTERS EXTEND BELOW THE WINDOW TO SKILLFULLY SCREEN AN UNATTRACTIVE HEATING VENT.

Above: A BEDROOM IN A FAMILY'S CONDOMINIUM HOME SEEMS MORE LIKE A STUDIO APARTMENT, GIVING A DAUGHTER A FIRST TASTE OF LIFE ON HER OWN. THE PAINTED CUPBOARD, UPHOLSTERED ARMCHAIR, AND COUNTRY-STYLE DAYBED ARE ALL INVESTMENT PIECES WITH A BRIGHT FUTURE. THE YOUNG LADY CAN TAKE THEM WITH HER TO A FUTURE HOME, OR THEY CAN REMAIN BEHIND TO FURNISH HER PARENTS' NEW GUEST ROOM.

Above: GROWN-UP AND JUVENILE TOUCHES INTERMINGLE FREELY IN THIS
ADOLESCENT'S ROOM, CREATING ITS ESSENTIAL CHARM. AT THE MOMENT, THREE SPRIGHTLY
BUNNIES PEEK OVER THE PILLOWS OF THE YOUNG PERSON'S BED. THESE CUTE
ANIMALS ARE BOUND TO DISAPPEAR IN A FEW YEARS' TIME, BUT THE BEAUTIFUL DRESSING
TABLE AND LONG ROSE DRAPES WILL LOOK AS ELEGANT AS EVER.

Above: THE CHILDREN'S GUEST ROOM AT GRANDMA'S HOUSE LETS SIBLINGS AND COUSINS ROOM TOGETHER IN ONE HAPPY DORMITORY. PLAID FLANNEL SHEETS AND MATCHING DUST RUFFLES COORDINATE THE MISMATCHED BEDS, WHICH WERE GATHERED TOGETHER FROM VARIOUS QUARTERS. THERE'S PLENTY OF ROOM ON THE FLOOR FOR OVERFLOW GUESTS WHO BRING THEIR SLEEPING BAGS.

Below: A PAINTED BEDROOM SET, ROSEBUD PRINT WALLPAPER, AND A FLORAL CARPET ENVELOP THIS ROOM WITH FEMININITY. POSITIONED NEAR THE WINDOW, AN UPHOLSTERED CHAISE LONGUE PERMITS RELAXED READING OR INDULGENT SNOOZES WITHOUT WORRY OF MUSSING UP THE BED. THE SWIVEL MIRROR'S SPIRE TOP IS A CONVENIENT SPOT FOR DISPLAYING THE OWNER'S FLOWER-TRIMMED HAT BETWEEN OUTINGS.

Above: FINDING PRIVACY TO SOCIALIZE WITH FRIENDS IS A SPECIAL NEED OF OLDER CHILDREN, ESPECIALLY WITHIN THE CONFINES OF A CITY APARTMENT. DAYBEDS TRANSFORM THIS BEDROOM INTO A SELF-CONTAINED SITTING ROOM. THEIR PLACEMENT OPPOSITE EACH OTHER FACILITATES CONVERSATION, WHILE THE PRESENCE OF A SECOND BED ALSO ALLOWS FOR AN OVERNIGHT GUEST. ASIDE FROM PROVIDING A WELL-LIT STUDY SPOT, THE LONG DESK COUNTER AT THE WINDOW CAN BE USED AS A BUFFET FOR REFRESHMENTS.

Opposite: A TENTLIKE DRAPE OVER A SCANDINAVIAN BOX BED PROVIDES THE SAME PLEASURE AS A CONVENTIONAL CANOPY BED. HIGH CEILINGS MAKE THE TENT EXCEPTIONALLY LOFTY, BUT THE SAME IDEA CAN BE ADAPTED FOR A CEILING OF LOWER HEIGHT AS WELL. THE ENTIRE ROOM IS SPARE AND SIMPLE, EVIDENCE OF A YOUNG PERSON'S MATURING TASTES.

Above: A DIMINUTIVE VANITY CAN BE THE FAVORITE SPOT OF A YOUNG GIRL EMBARKING UPON ADOLESCENCE, EXPERIMENTING WITH MAKEUP AND HAIRSTYLES. HAVING SPECIAL DRAWERS TO STORE JEWELRY, COSMETICS, AND TRINKETS IS NOT ONLY FUN, BUT HELPFUL IN KEEPING AN OTHERWISE TIDY ROOM FREE OF MISCELLANEOUS CLUTTER. PERCHED ON A NEARBY RADIATOR, A BELOVED CHIMP REMINDS ALL WHO ENTER THAT THIS STAGE OF LIFE IS NOT A COMPLETE DEPARTURE FROM CHILDHOOD, BUT RATHER A PERIOD OF TRANSITION.

Opposite: WHEN AN OLDER CHILD'S TWIN BED IS REPLACED BY A DOUBLE, IT MAY TAKE A LITTLE WORK TO ACCOMMODATE THE NEW, LARGER PIECE OF FURNITURE. HERE, THE SPACE PROBLEM HAS BEEN RESOLVED BY BACKING AN ANTIQUE DESK AGAINST THE FOOT OF A DOUBLE BED, ALLOWING BOTH PIECES TO FIT IN THE NARROW BEDROOM. **Above:** A TWIN BED, A NIGHTSTAND, AND OPEN SHELVING FOR BOOKS AND TROPHIES ARE PREDICTABLE FURNISHINGS IN AN ACTIVE BOY'S ROOM. THE SURPRISE FEATURE IS THE DEEP SHADE OF BLUE THAT COVERS THE WALLS, CREATING AN AIR OF BOLDNESS. CLEVERLY MASKING UNEVEN EDGES AT THE CEILING LINE, A SPORTS-MINDED WALLPAPER BORDER RUNS AROUND THE ROOM.

Above: FOR A TEENAGER WHO'D RATHER BE CAMPING THAN STUDYING, A BEDROOM WALL PAINTED WITH NATURE MURALS IS THE NEXT BEST THING. A REALISTIC WETLANDS SCENE AND TWO LEAFY TREES PROVIDE IMMEDIATE AMBIENCE RIGHT AT HOME. THE EXTRA PATTERN AND COLOR THAT A MURAL SUPPLIES HELP TO MAKE A SIMPLY FURNISHED ROOM APPEAR MORE DYNAMIC WITHOUT INTRODUCING OBJECTS THAT WOULD CLUTTER THE SPACE. **Right:** TROMPE L'OEIL PAINTING TURNS AN ORDINARY BEDROOM INTO A LOG CABIN INTERIOR. THE DECEPTION EXTENDS TO A RUGGED DENIM JACKET HANGING ON THE DOOR AND A DISHEVELED BOOKCASE. IN KEEPING WITH THE RUSTIC THEME, TWIN BEDS ARE APPROPRIATELY DRESSED IN LUMBERJACK'S PLAID FLANNEL.

Opposite: THE SHEER SIZE OF THIS SHARED ROOM ORIGINALLY OVERWHELMED THE TWIN BEDS AND MADE THEM SEEM

BORING AND BARRACKLIKE. TO BREAK UP THE RECTILINEAR MONOTONY, THE BEDS WERE TURNED ON AN ANGLE

AND TOPPED WITH EYE-POPPING BLACK-AND-WHITE SPREADS. THE NEW ARRANGEMENT STILL LEAVES PLENTY OF FLOOR SPACE

FOR ROLL-IN BICYCLE STORAGE. **Above, left:** BUILT-IN FURNITURE TAKES THE EDGE OFF A SPACE CRUNCH

IN A YOUNG TEENAGER'S SMALL BEDROOM. INSTEAD OF GOBBLING UP PRECIOUS FLOOR SPACE LIKE A TRADITIONAL DRESSER,

A TRIANGULAR CORNER CLOSET STACKED WITH SHELVES STORES THE TEEN'S EXTENSIVE WARDROBE ON A VERTICAL

AXIS. TO FACILITATE MOVEMENT WITHIN THE ROOM, THE CLOSET'S TRIANGULAR FOOTPRINT PERMITS A CLEAR, WIDE PATH TO

THE WINDOWED STUDY AREA INCORPORATED BEHIND THE PARTITION. USED FOR SLEEPING AS WELL AS LOUNGING,

A CARPETED PLATFORM TOPPED BY A SINGLE MATTRESS VISUALLY EXTENDS THE FLOOR SURFACE IN THIS COMPACT,

WELL-ORGANIZED SPACE. **Above, right:** STREAMLINED CONTEMPORARY FURNISHINGS—BED, DESK, CREDENZA,

DRESSER, AND LOUNGE CHAIRS—SUIT A BOY'S BACHELOR IMAGE. TO PRESERVE THE ROOM'S CLEAN, SLEEK STYLE,

SUPERFLUOUS ITEMS ARE STORED RATHER THAN DISPLAYED, LEAVING PLENTY OF UNCLUTTERED SPACE FOR ENTERTAINING GUESTS.

A YOUNG HOST CAN QUICKLY AND EASILY SET UP GUEST BEDS FOR HIS OVERNIGHT VISITORS BY UNFOLDING EACH

LOW-SLUNG, DUAL-PURPOSE LOUNGE CHAIR INTO A TWIN-SIZE MATTRESS.

APPENDIX: A CHILD'S ROOM CHECKLIST

Ideally, a child's room should be highly functional, teaming up a variety of elements, large and small. The checklist that follows highlights basic choices and considerations, and offers suggestions for conventional as well as novel decorating approaches.

BEDS

Beds for infants include bassinets, portable cribs, and full-size cribs—the last of these being the most expensive. It is important to choose a crib with a swing-down or swing-out gate so that caregivers don't have to bend over to pick up the baby, thereby risking back strain. Some cribs convert into toddler beds with guardrails to protect restless sleepers. Older children can graduate to single beds, bunk beds, loft/storage beds, or canopy beds. Trundle beds provide extra sleeping space for overnight guests or siblings sharing a room. Antique beds are appropriate as long as they are sturdy and free of lead paint (or of fumes from any paint remover or refinishing solution). *Do not lay an infant in an antique crib.* The slats may be spaced farther apart than is currently recommended, and the baby's head may get wedged between them.

STORAGE

The most important feature to consider when investing in children's storage is accessibility. Chests and interior closet fittings must be low enough so that children can reach their things and put them away easily. Drawers should have easy-to-grip handles and be free-gliding so that they can be opened and closed without a struggle. Deep slide-out baskets or cubbyholes are preferable to drawers for storing bulky clothing such as sweaters and sweatshirts. Low-hanging peg racks and clothes trees encourage children to hang up clothes that are worn frequently.

Portable multipurpose storage units are the best buy for children's rooms over the long term. Options include plastic or rubber bins with self-locking covers; freestanding steel, wood, or laminated shelving units; slide-out wire baskets; stackable plastic crates; and room dividers with large cubbyholes. Highly adaptable, these can hold anything from toys to books, can be rearranged as needed, and can be taken along to a new residence. Architectural storage units, though not readily portable, can be just as flexible in terms of what they contain. Options include built-in bookcases, window seats, and bed platforms with drawer or cupboard storage underneath and/or above. When choosing a storage unit for a child's room, examine it carefully for rough edges that could cause inadvertent injury, and make sure the unit is appropriate for the child's size and activities.

WORK SURFACES AND DESKS

Smooth, washable work surfaces are practical for all ages. For younger children, a low table with matching chairs is perfect for coloring, looking at books, assembling picture puzzles, and playing with other toys. Even if children end up sprawled on the floor for some of these activities, having a table-and-chair set available that's just their size enhances their sense of comfort and self-confidence.

Older children need larger work surfaces. Adjustable student-size drafting tables are suitable for many hobbies, from sewing to model making. Desk surfaces should be deep enough to allow room for a personal computer or a textbook and notebook. It is important to provide plenty of drawers so that the top surface can be cleared of papers, supplies, and other equipment if necessary.

LIGHTING

If possible, the rooms of infants and young children should receive plenty of natural light throughout the day. (Be sure, however, to protect infants from direct rays.) A soft overhead light or several lamps around the room are ample for evening, as long as extra task lighting is placed at desks and hobby areas. A bedside lamp is a must for nighttime reading. Night-lights and hall lights can be kept on or off, depending on the sleeping patterns of the individual child.

FLOORS

The typical floor surfaces for bedrooms are wood, vinyl tile, and carpet. Wood and vinyl tile have smooth, hard surfaces that are easy to clean and are ideal for young children's play. Either one can be quite comfortable as long as the home's heating system is adequate and the floors are not cold to the touch. Plush pile carpeting introduces a touch of luxury to the bedroom that many people, including older children, prefer. In an old or drafty house, carpeting may be the best option.

WALLS

Washable paints and wallpapers are the sensible choice for young children's rooms. Themed wallpapers with matching border prints can be quite attractive and fun, but be aware that they may limit rather than expand your decorating options. The child will certainly outgrow these wall treatments sooner than a solid-color paint finish. If you decide to commission a hand-painted mural, try to select a theme that has staying power. Large bulletin boards are a must for keeping track of artwork, photographs, greeting cards, report cards, party invitations, and other paper items. Remember to mount all bulletin boards at the child's eye level.

SOURCES

DESIGNERS

(pages 2 and 50)
Summer House for Kids
San Francisco, CA
(415) 383-6690

(page 6)
Inter-Ikea Systems B.V.,
  Ikea U.S.
Plymouth Meeting, PA
(215) 834-0180

(pages 9 and 16)
Bill Caroll
Model Homes Interiors
Beltsville, MD
(301) 937-6145

(page 12, top)
Katherine Stephens
New York, NY
(212) 593-1109

(page 12, bottom)
Susan Black
Periwinkles
Medford, MA
(617) 623-1980

(pages 14 and 65)
Bonnie Siracusa
Great Neck, NY
(516) 482-3349

(pages 19 and 42)
Judith Cohen Interiors
Scarsdale, NY
(914) 723-3627

(pages 21 and 34,
  top and bottom)
Rubén de Saavedra
New York, NY
(212) 759-2892

(page 22, bottom)
Marcia Conors
Growing Interior Design
Canton, MA
(617) 828-3213

(page 23)
Judith Slaughter
Alpharetta, GA
(404) 594-1768

(page 26)
Lisa Furse
Lisbon Interiors
Chicago, IL
(708) 295-1444

(page 28, top)
Michael Smith
Los Angeles, CA
(310) 278-9046

(page 28, bottom)
Ronald Bricke & Associates
New York, NY
(212) 472-9006

(page 29, top)
Charles Riley
New York, NY
(212) 206-8395

(pages 30 and 57)
Sara Olesker Ltd.
Chicago, IL
(312) 248-9100

(pages 31 and 61)
Joe Terrell
Los Angeles, CA
(213) 469-8044

(page 32, top)
D'Image Associates
Saddle River, NJ
(201) 934-5420

(page 32, bottom)
Izhar Patkin
New York, NY
(212) 254-3056

(page 35)
Susan Reichhart
S.H. Reichhart Interiors
Fallston, MD
(410) 557-9983

(page 36)
Claudia Skylar, Architect
Chicago, IL
(312) 935-0984

(page 38, left)
KHR Design
New York, NY
(212) 861-4805

(page 40)
Steven Ehrlich, Architect
Los Angeles, CA
(310) 828-6700

(page 41, top)
Susan Fredman
Lake Forest, IL
(708) 831-1419

(page 43)
Karen Berkemeyen
Greenwich, CT
(203) 869-8800

(page 45)
Adam Tihany
Tihany International
New York, NY
(212) 505-2360

(page 46)
Connie Driscoll Interior
Design
Nantucket, MA
(617) 259-0878

(pages 48 and 56, top)
Suzanne Kelly
New York, NY
(212) 988-7721

(page 49, top)
Carole Kaplan
Two by Two Interior Design
Andover, MA
(508) 470-3131

(pages 49, bottom, and 64)
Debby Smith
Nantucket, MA
(508) 465-2435

(page 56, bottom)
Peg Heron
Classic Galleries
Huntington, NY
(516) 427-1045

(page 58)
Fred Cannon, Jr.
New York, NY
(212) 753-5600

(page 59, bottom)
Ann Fitzpatrick Brown
Country Curtains
Stockbridge, MA
(413) 298-5565

(page 63)
Terry Irvin
Dacula, GA
(404) 995-0165

(page 66)
Caledonian
Chicago, IL
(708) 446-6566

(page 67, left and right)
Vassa
The Vassa Group
Chicago, IL
(312) 664-5800

PHOTOGRAPHY CREDITS

© Peter Aaron/Esto
Photographics: 37
© Otto Baitz/Esto
Photographics: 17
© Grey Crawford: 31, 40,
61
© Mark Darley/Esto
Photographics: 2, 50
© Daniel Eifert: Design:
Katherine Stephens: 12
top; Design: Rubén de
Saavedra: 21, 34 all
© Phillip H. Ennis
Photography: 11, 15
bottom, 28 bottom, 48,
53, 54, 56 top
© Feliciano: 41 bottom, 58
© Scott Frances/Esto
Photographics: 30, 32
bottom, 38 left, 57
© Michael Garland: Design:
Lauren Elia: 18; Design:
Fred Fisher: 29 bottom
© Tria Giovan: 22 top, 29
top, 33 top
© Jeff Goldberg/Esto
Photographics: 39, 59 top
© David Henderson/Eric
Roth Studio: Design: Debby
Smith: 49 bottom, 64
© Nancy Hill: 44; Design:
Judith Cohen Interiors:
19, 42

© Inter IKEA Systems B.V.: 6
© Dennis Krukowski: 59
bottom; Design: D'Image,
Saddle River, N.J.: 32 top
© Tim Lee: 43
© Michael Mundy: Design:
Michael Smith: 28 top
© Peter Paige: Design:
Adam Tihany: 45
© Robert Perron: 38 right;
Design: Ted Pappas: 52
© Eric Roth: 12 bottom, 13
all, 46, 51, 62; Design:
Marcia Conors: 22 bot-
tom; Design: Carole
Kaplan/Two by Two
Interior Design: 49 top
© Bill Rothschild: 10, 14,
15 top, 56 bottom, 65
© J. Brough Schamp/TAB
Stock: 35
© Schulenburg/The Interior
World: 24, 25; Design:
Andrew Wadsworth: 20,
33 bottom, 60; Design:
Sissi Edmiston: 27
© Ernest Silva/FPG
International: 47
© Ron Solomon/TAB Stock:
9, 16
© Jessie Walker Associates:
26, 36, 41 top, 66, 67 all

INDEX